Decodable Takehome Books

Level 1
Practice Books 1-48

A Division of The McGraw-Hill Companies

Columbus, Ohio

www.sra4kids.com

SRA/McGraw-Hill

A Division of The McGraw·Hill Companies

Contents

About the Takehome Books

The *SRA Open Court Reading Decodable Books* allow your students to apply their knowledge of phonic elements to read simple, engaging texts. Each story supports instruction in a new phonic element and incorporates elements and words that have been learned earlier.

The students can fold and staple the pages of each *Decodable Takehome Book* to make books of their own to keep and read. We suggest that you keep extra sets of the stories in your classroom for the children to reread.

How to make a Takehome Book

1. Tear out the pages you need.

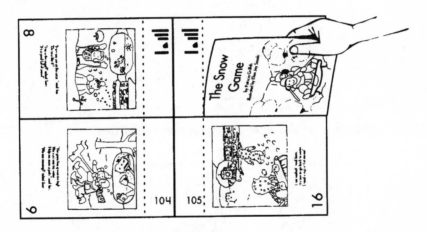

2. Place pages 4 and 5, and pages 2 and 7 faceup.

3. Place pages 4 and 5 on top of pages 2 and 7.

4. Fold along the center line.

5. Check to make sure the pages are in order.

6. Staple the pages along the fold.

Just to let you know...

A message from _____

Help your child discover the joy of independent reading with *SRA Open Court Reading.* From time to time your child will bring home his or her very own *Decodable Takehome Books* to share with you. With your help, these stories can give your child important reading practice and a joyful shared reading experience.

You may want to set aside a few minutes every evening to read these stories together. Here are some suggestions you may find helpful:

- Do not expect your child to read each story perfectly, but concentrate on sharing the book together.
- Participate by doing some of the reading.
- Talk about the stories as you read, give lots of encouragement, and watch as your child becomes more fluent throughout the year!

Learning to read takes lots of practice. Sharing these stories is one way that your child can gain that valuable practice. Encourage your child to keep the *Decodable Takehome Books* in a special place. This collection will make a library of books that your child can read and reread. Take the time to listen to your child read from his or her library. Just a few moments of shared reading each day can give your child the confidence needed to excel in reading.

Children who read every day come to think of reading as a pleasant, natural part of life. One way to inspire your child to read is to show that reading is an important part of your life by letting him or her see you reading books, magazines, newspapers, or any other materials. Another good way to show that you value reading is to share a *Decodable Takehome Book* with your child each day.

Successful reading experiences allow children to be proud of their new-found reading ability. Support your child with interest and enthusiasm about reading. You won't regret it!

SRA Open Court Reading

On a Mat

Practice Book 1

SRA

A Division of The McGraw-Hill Companies

Columbus, Ohio

Tam sat.
Sam sat.
Matt sat.
I sat on a mat.

www.sra4kids.com

SRA/McGraw-Hill

A Division of The McGraw-Hill Companies

Copyright © 2002 by SRA/McGraw-Hill.

Printed in the United States of America.

Send all inquiries to:
SRA/McGraw-Hill
8787 Orion Place
Columbus, OH 43240-4027

Tam sat.
Tam sat on a mat.

Tam is on a mat.

3

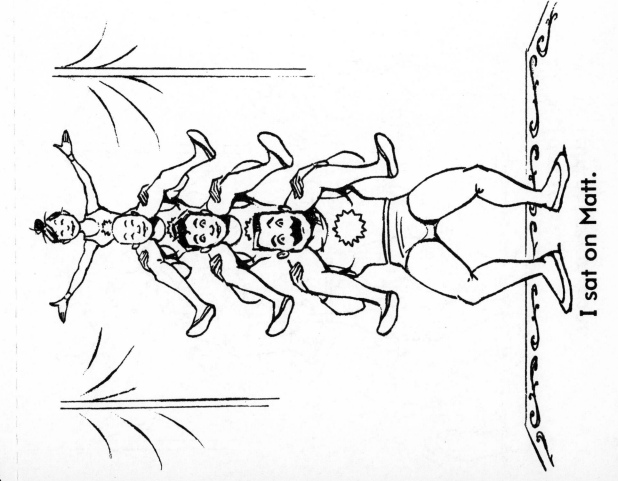

I sat on Matt.

6

Sam sat on Tam.

Matt sat on Sam.

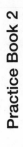

SRA OPEN COURT READING

Tam Has Ham

Practice Book 2

SRA

A Division of The McGraw-Hill Companies

Columbus, Ohio

Tam has ham.

Tam has ham.

Tam sat and sat and sat.

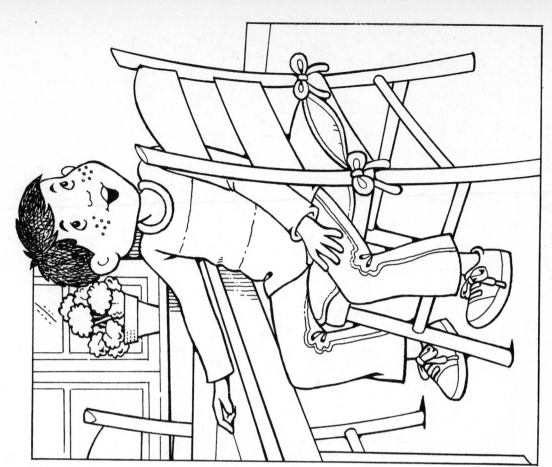

Sam sat.

Tam sat.

4

Sam sat at a

table

.

Sam has ham.

5

SRA Open Court Reading

Pam and Hap

Practice Book 3

SRA

A Division of The McGraw-Hill Companies

Columbus, Ohio

17

Hap sat on Pam!

Is Hap in a hat?
Hap was in a hat.

Hap is in a hat.

3

Pam taps a hat.
Tap, tap, tap, tap.

6

4

A hat is on Pam.

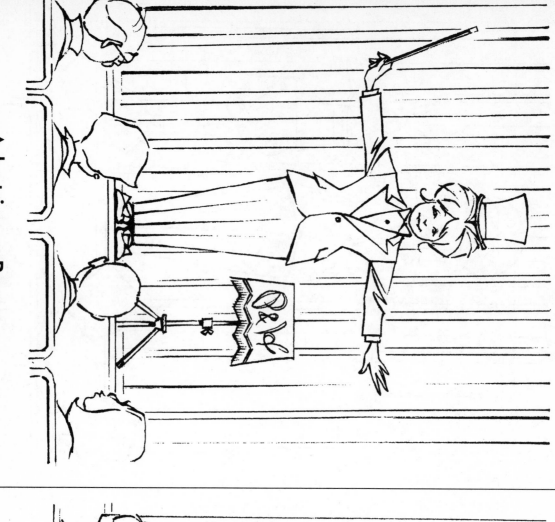

Pam pats a hat.
Pat, pat, pat, pat.

5

Tim Hit It

SRA Open Court Reading

Practice Book 4

SRA

A Division of The McGraw-Hill Companies
Columbus, Ohio

Tim's hit is in Pam's mitt.

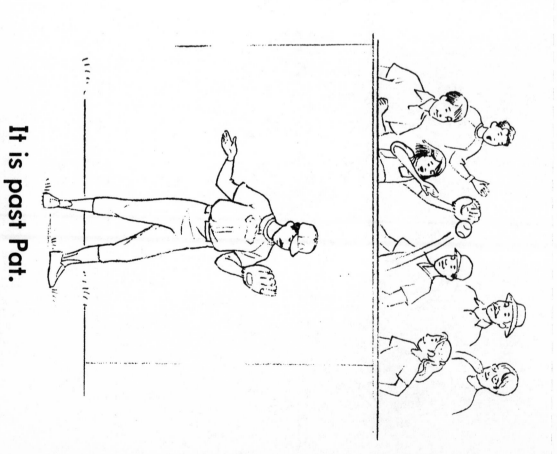

It is past Pat.
Tim's hit is past Pat.

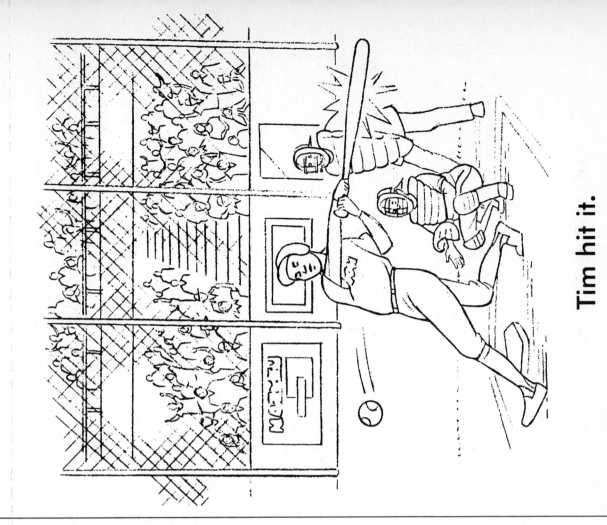

Tim hit it.

3

It hit the tip.
It hit the mitt's tip.

6

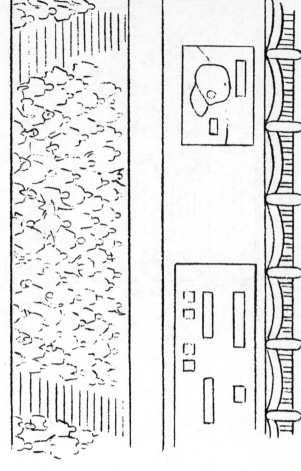

Tim hit it at Pat.

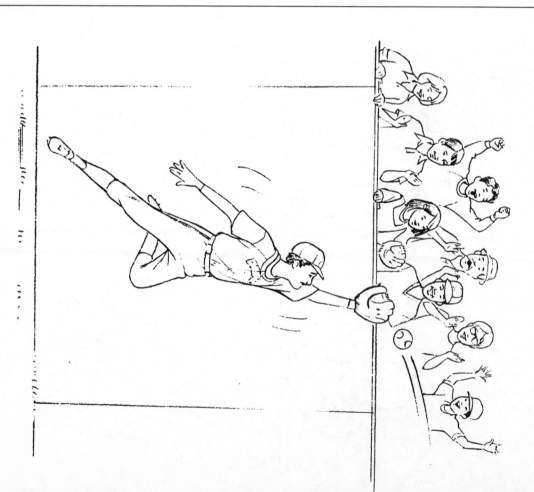

Is it in Pat's mitt?

SRA Open Court READING

Nat

Practice Book 5

SRA

A Division of The McGraw-Hill Companies

Columbus, Ohio

Nat naps and naps.

Nat sits.

Nat naps.

An ant sits by Nat.
An ant taps Nat.

6

4

Nan hits a tin pan.
Nat naps and naps.

Pam tips a tin pan.
Nat naps and naps and naps.

5

SRA OPEN COURT READING

Pals

Practice Book 6

SRA

A Division of The McGraw-Hill Companies

Columbus, Ohio

Tip and Lin are pals.

www.sra4kids.com

SRA/McGraw-Hill

A Division of The McGraw-Hill Companies

Copyright © 2002 by SRA/McGraw-Hill.

Printed in the United States of America.

Send all inquiries to:
SRA/McGraw-Hill
8787 Orion Place
Columbus, OH 43240-4027

2

Tip's hat is on Lin.

Tip is Lin's pal.
Lin is Tip's pal.

3

The pin is on Tip's hat.

6

4

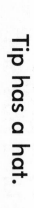

Tip has a hat.

Lin has a pin.

5

SRA Open Court Reading

Pam's Hill

Practice Book 7

SRA

A Division of The McGraw-Hill Companies

Columbus, Ohio

Halt, Pam!
Pam is on the ham on the hill.
It is Pam's ham.
Pam's ham is in Pam.

8

www.sra4kids.com

SRA/McGraw-Hill

A Division of The McGraw-Hill Companies

Copyright © 2002 by SRA/McGraw-Hill.

All rights reserved. Except as permitted under the United States Copyright Act, no part of this publication may be reproduced or distributed in any form or by any means, or stored in a database or retrieval system, without prior written permission from the publisher.

Printed in the United States of America.

Send all inquiries to:
SRA/McGraw-Hill
8787 Orion Place
Columbus, OH 43240-4027

Pam is still on the hill.

Ham is on Pam's hill.

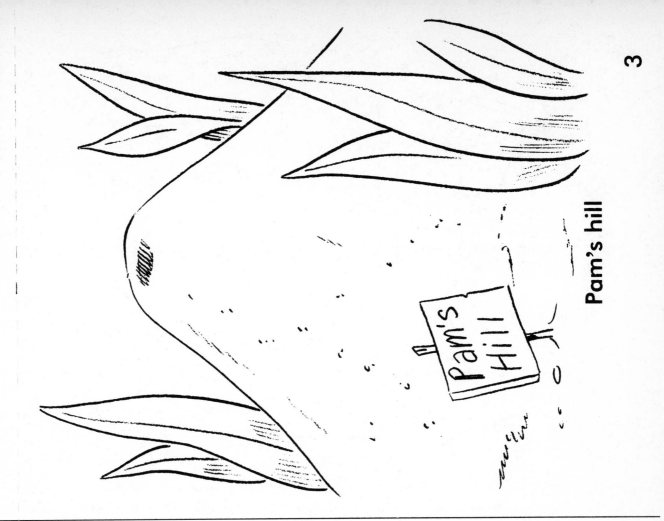

Pam's hill

Pam is on the tall hill.

Pam is small.

4

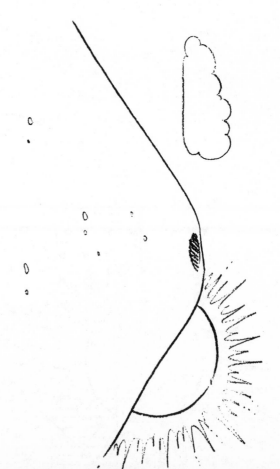

The hill is tall.
It is too tall.

5

SRA Open Court Reading

Dad's Mitt

Practice Book 8

SRA

A Division of *The McGraw-Hill Companies*

Columbus, Ohio

Tad hit.
Tad's hit is in Dad's mitt on
Dan's hand!

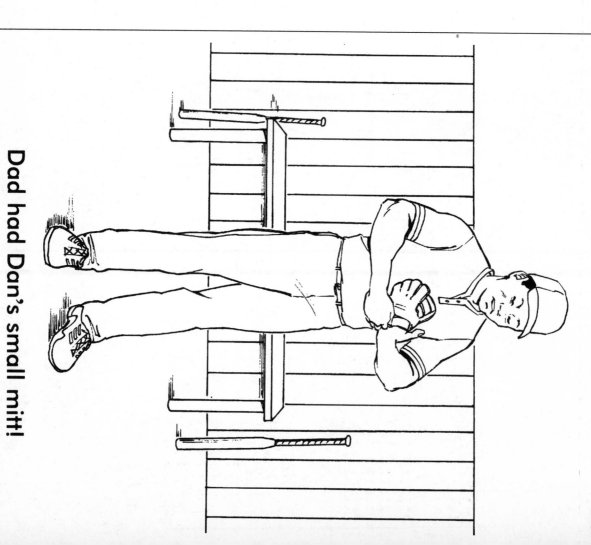

Dad had Dan's small mitt!

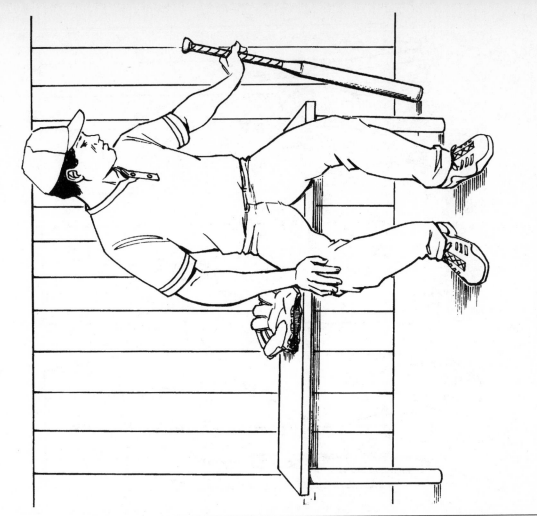

Dad had a mitt.

3

Dan had Dad's mitt on his small hand!

6

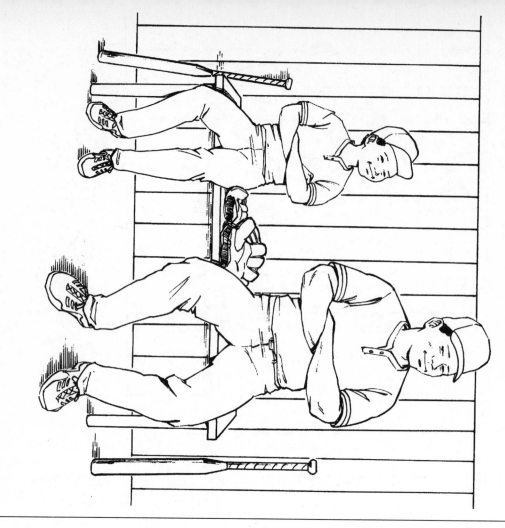

Dan had a mitt.

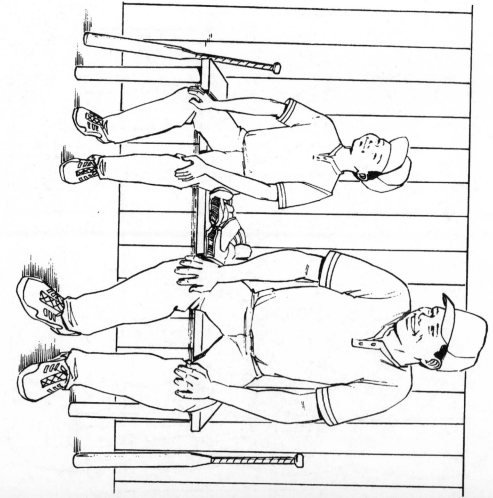

Dan had a small hand.

SRA OPEN COURT READING

Tom and Pop

Practice Book 9

SRA

A Division of The McGraw-Hill Companies

Columbus, Ohio

41

Tom and Pop are not hot.

8

2

The pot is on top.
The pot is on Pop.

7

Tom is hot.

3

Tom's pop has a pot.

6

Tom hops in the pond.

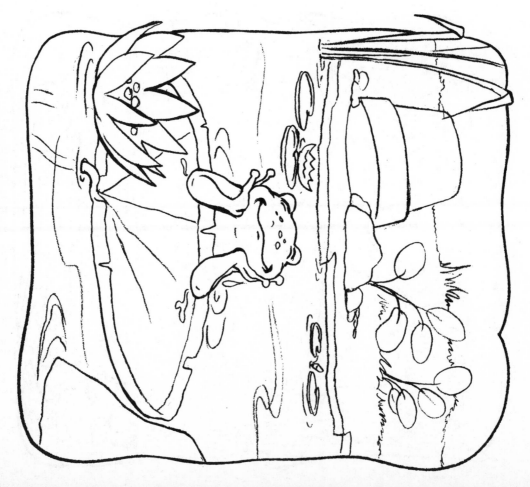

The pond is not hot.

SRA Open Court Reading

Bop!

Practice Book 10

SRA
A Division of The McGraw-Hill Companies
Columbus, Ohio

45

Todd did not nab the ball.
Too bad, Todd.

8

www.sra4kids.com

SRA/McGraw-Hill

A Division of The McGraw-Hill Companies

Copyright © 2002 by SRA/McGraw-Hill.

All rights reserved. Except as permitted under the United States Copyright Act, no part of this publication may be reproduced or distributed in any form or by any means, or stored in a database or retrieval system, without prior written permission from the publisher.

Printed in the United States of America.

Send all inquiries to:
SRA/McGraw-Hill
8787 Orion Place
Columbus, OH 43240-4027

2

Babs is still at bat.
Bop!

7

Babs is at bat.

3

Todd cannot nab the ball.

6

Babs hits the ball.
Bop!

Can Todd nab the ball?

SRA Open Court Reading

Cal's Cap

Practice Book 11

SRA

A Division of The McGraw-Hill Companies

Columbus, Ohio

A cat spots Cal's cap.
The cat can stop Cal's cap!

8

Who can stop Cal's cap?

Cal has a cap.

3

A man in a cab cannot stop Cal's cap.

6

51

4

Can Cal's mom stop the cap?

Cal's mom cannot stop Cal's cap.

5

53

SRA Open Court Reading

The Snack

Practice Book 12

A Division of The McGraw-Hill Companies

Columbus, Ohio

Nick is back.
Where is his snack?

8

2

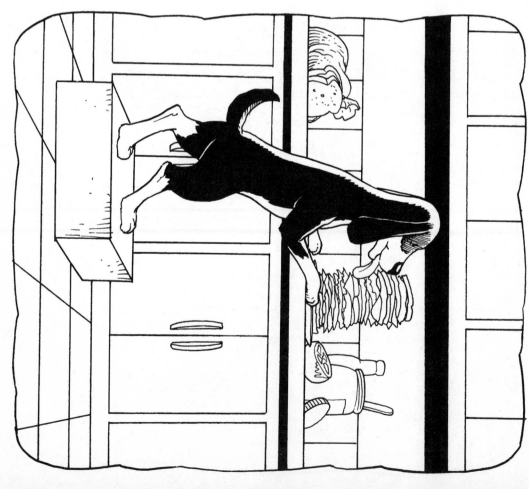

Socks licks Nick's snack.

7

Nick makes a snack.

3

Socks is on Nick's block.

6

4

Nick stacks a snack.

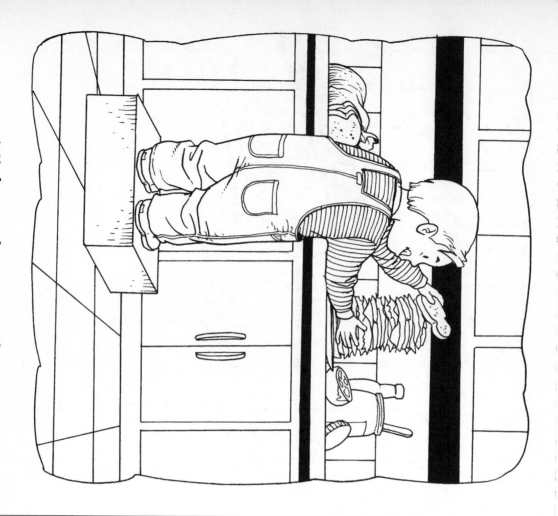

Socks spots Nick's snack.

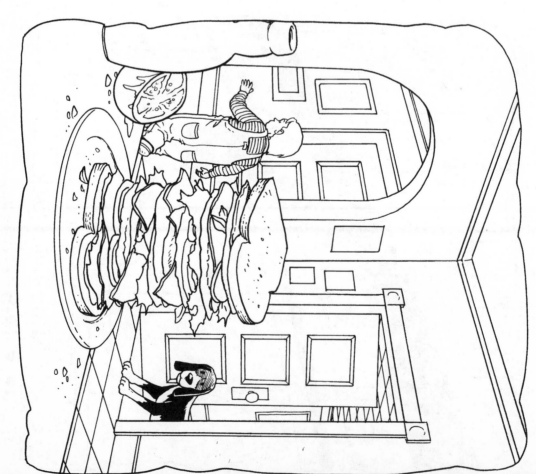

5

SRA OPEN COURT READING

Practice Book 13

SRA

A Division of The McGraw-Hill Companies

Columbus, Ohio

Rick and Rob

Rob licks Rick.
Rob is there.
Rob is by Rick.

8

Rick sprints and trips.

SRA Open Court Reading

Rick sits and prints.

3

Rob licks Rick.
Rick cannot pick a trick.

6

Rob licks Rick.
Rick cannot print.

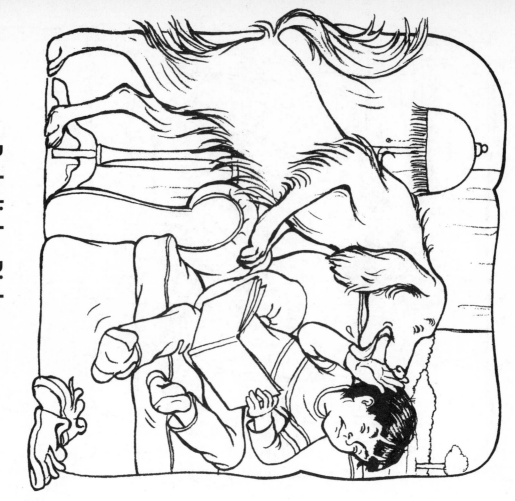

Rick sits and picks a trick.

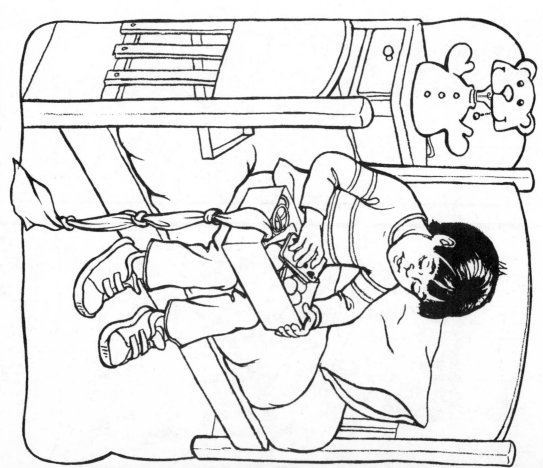

Ann Hunts for Nuts

SRA Open Court Reading

Practice Book 14

A Division of The McGraw-Hill Companies

Columbus, Ohio

But Nan has bad luck, too.

www.sra4kids.com

SRA/McGraw-Hill

A Division of The McGraw-Hill Companies

Copyright © 2002 by SRA/McGraw-Hill.

Send all inquiries to:
SRA/McGraw-Hill
8787 Orion Place
Columbus, OH 43240-4027

2

Nan picks up Ann's nuts!

Ann hunts for nuts.

3

Ann has bad luck.

6

Nan hunts for nuts.

The sun is hot, but Ann still hunts.

65

SRA Open Court Reading

Stuck!

Practice Book 15

SRA

A Division of The McGraw-Hill Companies

Columbus, Ohio

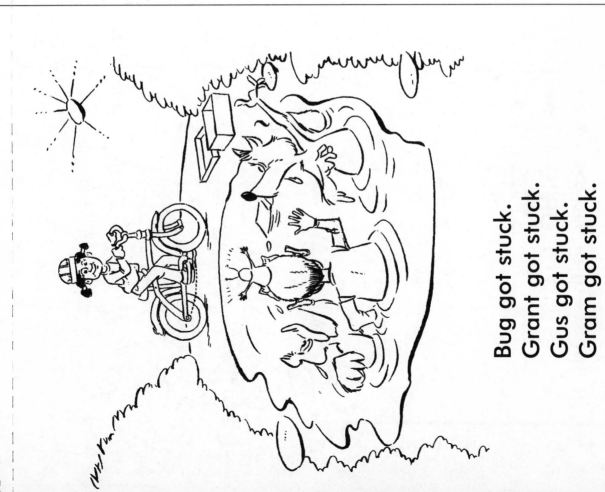

Bug got stuck.
Grant got stuck.
Gus got stuck.
Gram got stuck.

www.sra4kids.com

SRA/McGraw-Hill

A Division of The McGraw-Hill Companies

Copyright © 2002 by SRA/McGraw-Hill.

All rights reserved. Except as permitted under the United States Copyright Act, no part of this publication may be reproduced or distributed in any form or by any means, or stored in a database or retrieval system, without prior written permission from the publisher.

Printed in the United States of America.

Send all inquiries to:
SRA/McGraw-Hill
8787 Orion Place
Columbus, OH 43240-4027

No! No!
SPLAT!
GLUG! GLUG!
All are in the mud!

Bug got stuck in the mud.
Glug! Glug!

3

Gram has a lid!
Grab the lid!
Tug on the lid.

6

Bug and Grant got stuck in the mud.

4

Bug and Grant and Gus got stuck in the mud.

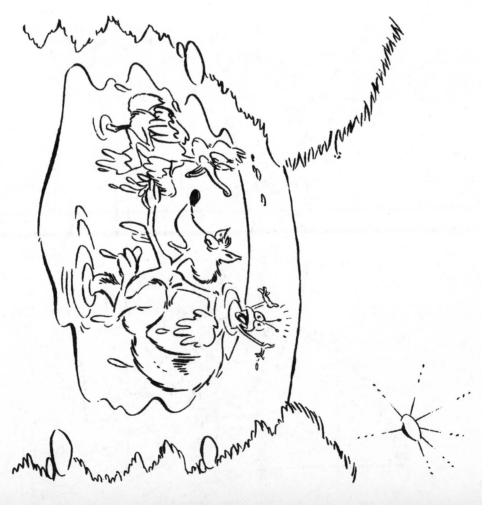

5

SRA Open Court Reading

Just Jam

Practice Book 16

A Division of The McGraw-Hill Companies
Columbus, Ohio

"Yes, Jack is a jam man," said Jan.

8

www.sra4kids.com

SRA/McGraw-Hill

A Division of The McGraw-Hill Companies

Printed in the United States of America.

Send all inquiries to:
SRA/McGraw-Hill
8787 Orion Place
Columbus, OH 43240-4027

2

"Jam in a jug? Just jam in a jug?" said Jim.

7

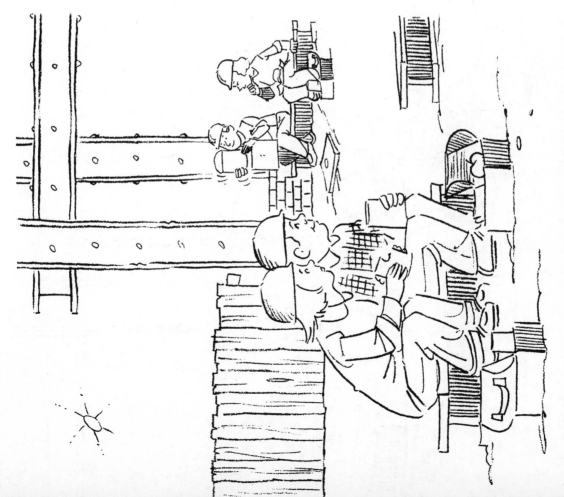

"Did Jill pack a snack?" said Jim.

3

"Yes, jam in a jug," said Jan.

6

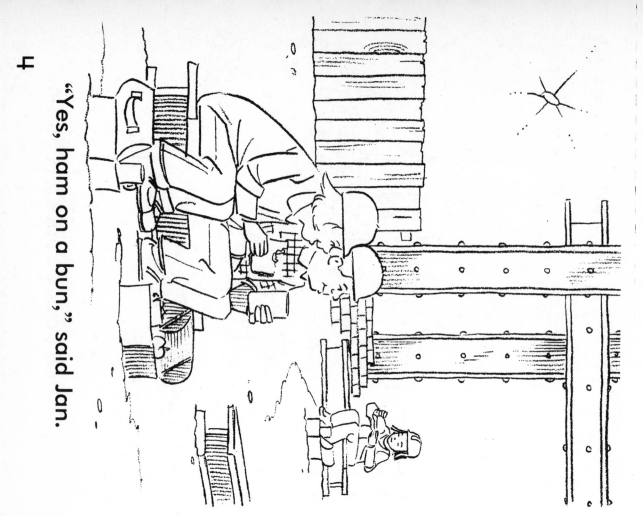

"Yes, ham on a bun," said Jan.

4

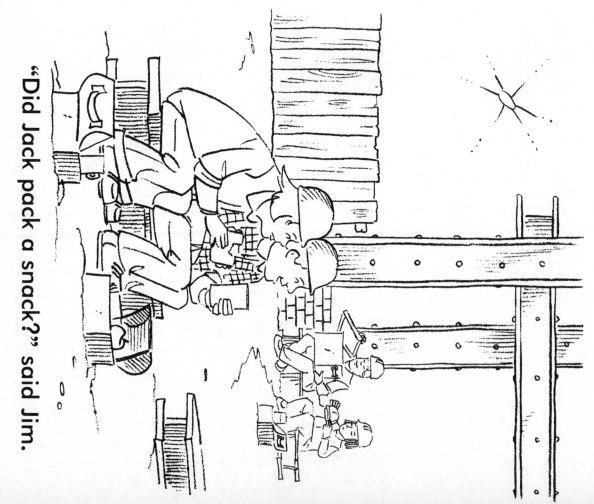

"Did Jack pack a snack?" said Jim.

5

SRA Open Court Reading

Madge

Practice Book 17

SRA
A Division of The McGraw-Hill Companies
Columbus, Ohio

The bus can budge.
But Madge cannot.

Madge put gas in the bus.

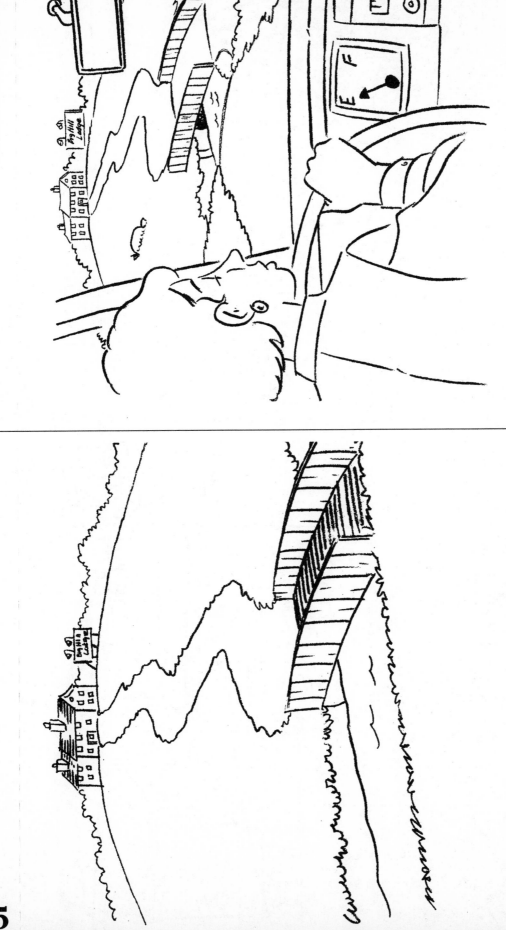

"This bus cannot budge," said Madge.
"It has no gas."

3

Madge ran past the lodge and down
the hill. Madge ran on the bridge and
up the ridge.

6

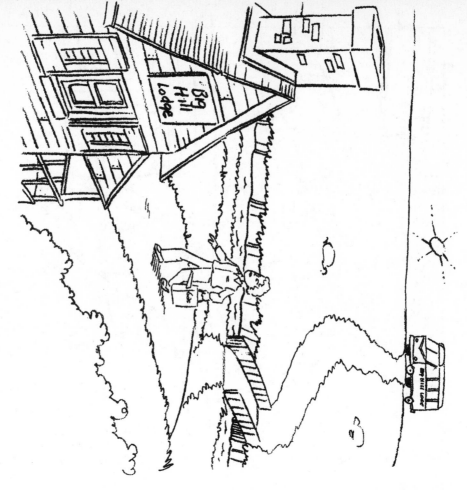

Madge ran down a ridge to a bridge.
Madge ran on a bridge to a hill.
Madge ran up a hill to a lodge.

4

At the lodge, Madge had to stop.
Madge got gas.

5

SRA Open Court Reading

Fran's Fudge

Practice Book 18

A Division of The McGraw-Hill Companies

Columbus, Ohio

Fudge can fit in Fran.
Fran had all the fudge.

www.sra4kids.com

SRA/McGraw-Hill

A Division of The McGraw-Hill Companies

Send all inquiries to:
SRA/McGraw-Hill
8787 Orion Place
Columbus, OH 43240-4027

2

If fudge cannot fit in a fridge, where can it fit?

7

Can Fran fit his fudge in a fridge?
Fran cannot judge.

3

Can it fit if a ham is there?
Can the fudge fit?
The fudge cannot fit.

6

4

The fudge cannot fit.

Can it fit if a jug is on top?
Can the fudge fit?
The fudge cannot fit.

5

SRA Open Court Reading

The Horn

Practice Book 19

SRA

A Division of The McGraw-Hill Companies

Columbus, Ohio

81

Mort acts fast.
Mort grabs a corncob.
He puts the corn in the horn.

8

www.sra4kids.com

SRA/McGraw-Hill

A Division of The McGraw-Hill Companies

Copyright © 2002 by SRA/McGraw-Hill.

All rights reserved. Except as permitted under the United States Copyright Act, no part of this publication may be reproduced or distributed in any form or by any means, or stored in a database or retrieval system, without prior written permission from the publisher.

Printed in the United States of America.

Send all inquiries to:
SRA/McGraw-Hill
8787 Orion Place
Columbus, OH 43240-4027

2

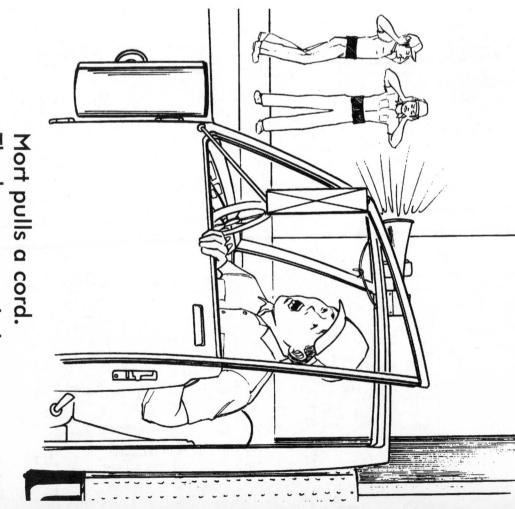

Mort pulls a cord.
The horn cannot stop.
It is stuck.

7

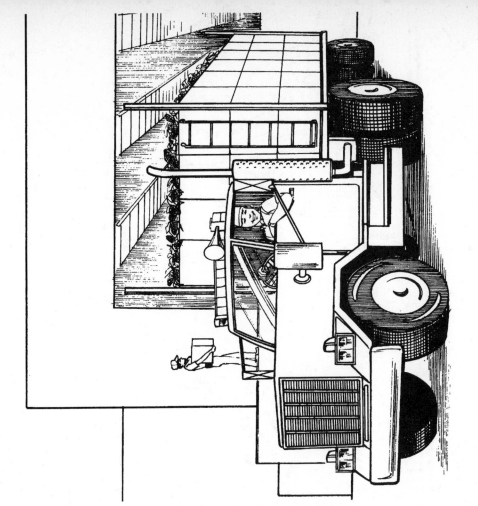

Mort is big.
His truck is big.
Its horn is big.

3

Mort has a plan.

6

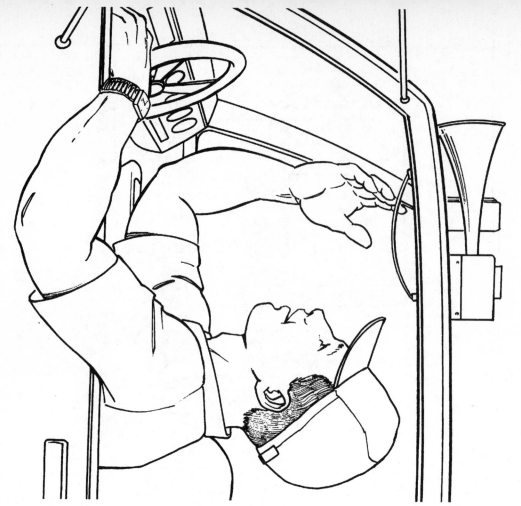

4

If Mort pulls a cord, the horn will blast.

Mort pulls a cord.
It is torn.
The horn cannot blast.

5

SRA Open Court Reading

Big Ted Is Best

Practice Book 20

SRA

A Division of The McGraw-Hill Companies

Columbus, Ohio

"Big Ted is Best"

★Jets★

I am Brent.
I am a Red Hen.
I am sad Big Ted is a Jet.

8

www.sra4kids.com

SRA/McGraw-Hill

A Division of The McGraw-Hill Companies

Send all inquiries to:
SRA/McGraw-Hill
8787 Orion Place
Columbus, OH 43240-4027

2

I am Ned.
I can get a Big Ted hit with a net.
I am glad Big Ted is a Jet.

7

Big Ted is a Jet.
Big Ted is the best Jet.

3

I am Meg.
I sell Jet stuff.
I am glad Big Ted is a Jet.

6

4

I am Jen.
I am a Jet fan.
I am glad Big Ted is a Jet.

I am Len.
I am a Jet.
Big Ted is the best.
I am glad Big Ted is a Jet.

5

SRA Open Court Reading

Fred and Jen Jumped

Practice Book 21

SRA

A Division of The McGraw-Hill Companies

Columbus, Ohio

Jen flipped.
Fred rested.

www.sra4kids.com

SRA/McGraw-Hill

A Division of The McGraw-Hill Companies

Copyright © 2002 by SRA/McGraw-Hill.

Printed in the United States of America.

Send all inquiries to:
SRA/McGraw-Hill
8787 Orion Place
Columbus, OH 43240-4027

Fred hopped.
Jen hopped.

Fred led Jen in a new sport.
Fred jumped.
Jen jumped.

3

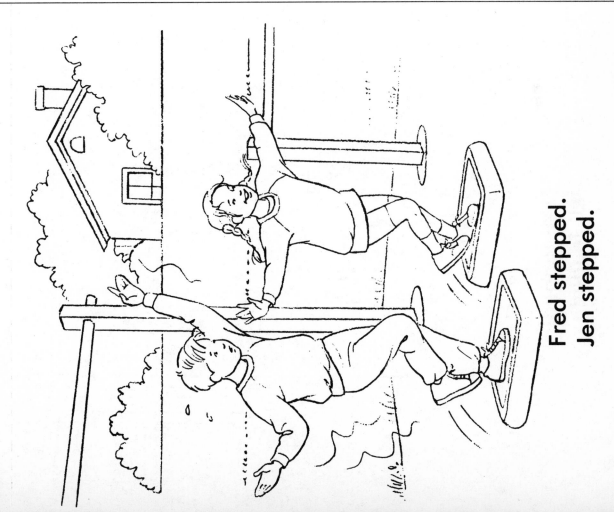

Fred stepped.
Jen stepped.

6

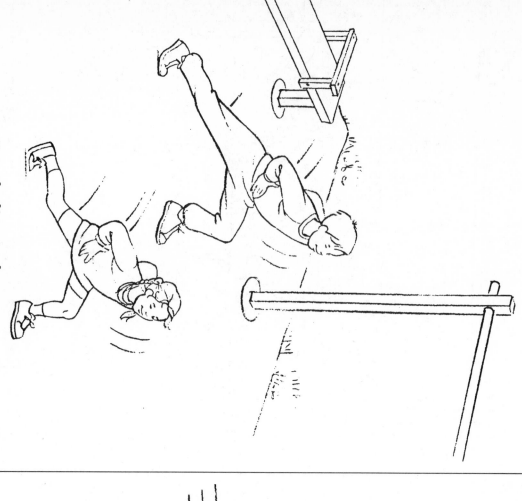

Fred dipped.
Jen dipped.

Fred jogged.
Jen jogged.

93

SRA OPEN COURT READING

Fred

Practice Book 22

SRA

A Division of The McGraw-Hill Companies

Columbus, Ohio

"Who wants my stuff?" Fred sniffed.

8

www.sra4kids.com

SRA/McGraw-Hill

A Division of The McGraw-Hill Companies

Send all inquiries to:
SRA/McGraw-Hill
8787 Orion Place
Columbus, OH 43240-4027

"Fig, Pat Pig?" called Fred.
"Not figs!" puffed Pat Pig.

"Ham, Sam Clam?" called Fred.
"Not ham," clicked Sam Clam.

3

"Melted fudge, Judge Jed?" called Fred.
"Not melted fudge," huffed Judge Jed.

6

"Grab a top hat, Bill Bat," said Fred.
"No top hats!" snapped Bill Bat.

4

"Jump in the jug, Ben Bug," said Fred.
"It's snug as a rug."
"No jug," grumped Ben Bug.

5

SRA OPEN COURT READING

Max Can Fix It

Practice Book 23

SRA

A Division of The McGraw-Hill Companies

Columbus, Ohio

1. Fix a box ☑
2. Rub a sax ☑
3. Fix a fox

2

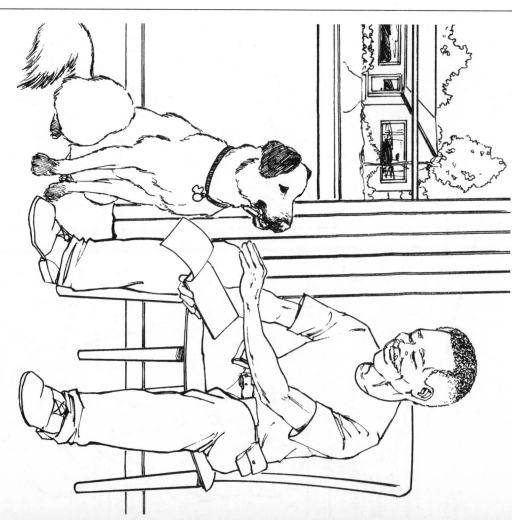

Last, Max can list the stuff he fixed.
Rex can help Max.

7

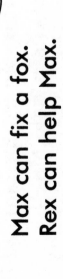

Max can fix stuff.
Rex can help Max.

3

Max can fix a fox.
Rex can help Max.

6

4

Max can fix a box.
Rex can help Max.

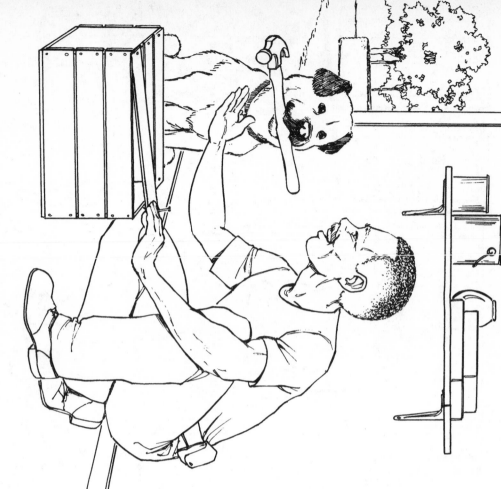

Next Max can rub a sax.
Rex can help Max.

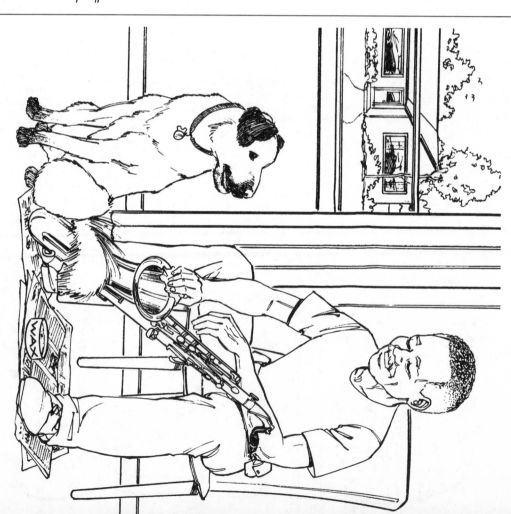

5

Liz

Practice Book 24

A Division of The McGraw-Hill Companies
Columbus, Ohio

Zap! Liz has a bug for a snack.

8

2

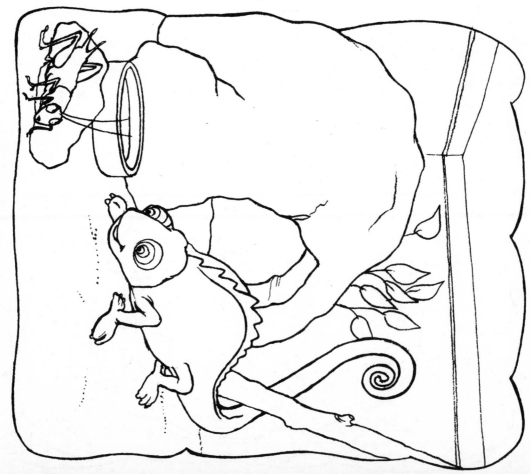

Liz can zap a bug.

7

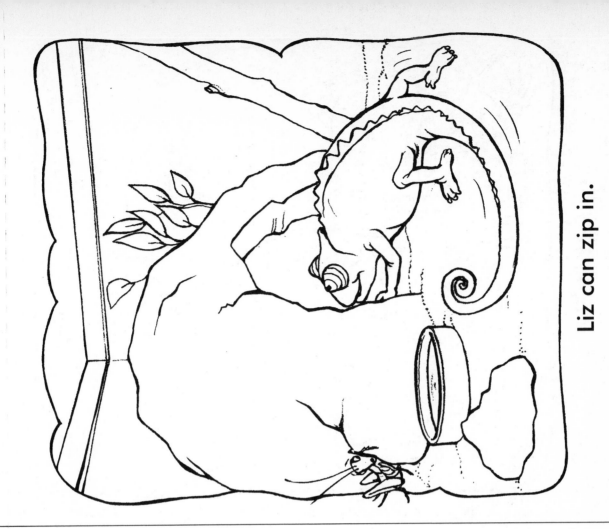

Liz can zip in.

3

Liz can zigzag down.

6

4

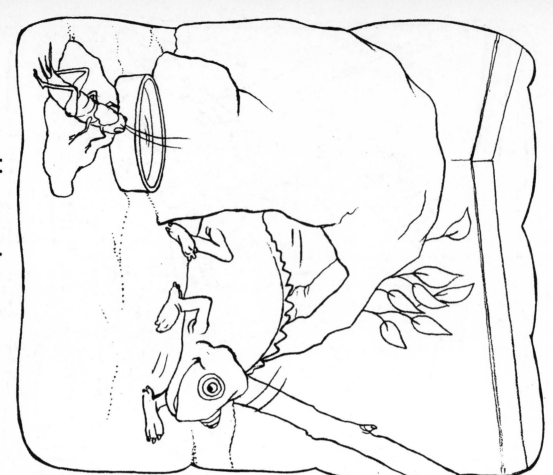

Liz can zip out.

Liz can zigzag up.

5

SRA OPEN COURT READING

Fuzz on a Cuff

Practice Book 25

SRA

A Division of The McGraw-Hill Companies
Columbus, Ohio

Mom picked at the fuzz on Buzz's cuff.

8

www.sra4kids.com

SRA/McGraw-Hill

A Division of The McGraw-Hill Companies

Copyright © 2002 by SRA/McGraw-Hill.

Printed in the United States of America.

Send all inquiries to:
SRA/McGraw-Hill
8787 Orion Place
Columbus, OH 43240-4027

What can Buzz do with the fuzz?

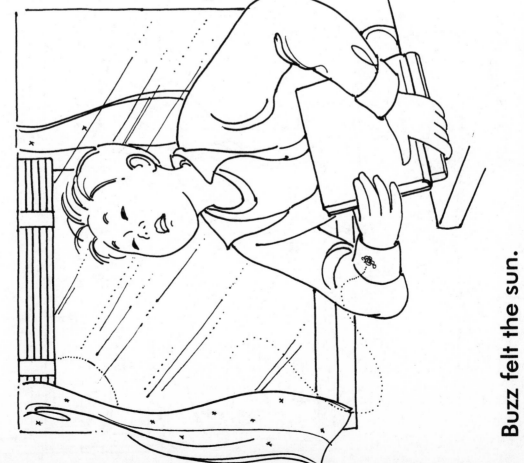

Buzz picked at the fuzz on his cuff.

3

Buzz felt the sun.
The fuzz landed back on Buzz's cuff.

6

4

Buzz had an egg.
The fuzz landed back on Buzz's cuff.

Buzz sipped.
Buzz picked at the fuzz on his cuff.

5

SRA Open Court Reading

Don and Jim

Practice Book 26

A Division of *The McGraw-Hill Companies*

Columbus, Ohio

Mom tells Jim to scrub his hands.
Mom tells Jim, "Do not get mud on Don!"

8

2

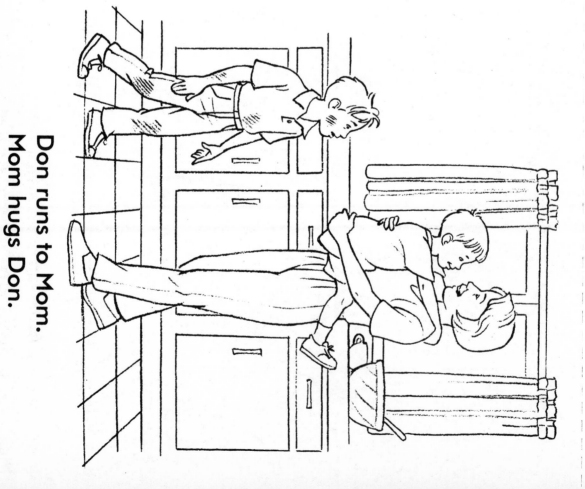

Don runs to Mom.
Mom hugs Don.

Don digs in the mud.
Jim fills it in.

3

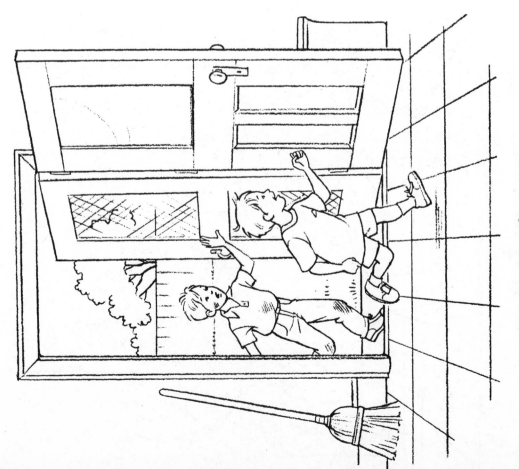

Don zigs and zags.
Jim runs to get Don.

6

4

Don has mud on his hands.
Jim scrubs Don's hands.

Don hugs Duff.
Jim gets rid of Duff.

5

113

SRA OPEN COURT READING

Zip the Tug

Practice Book 27

SRA

A Division of The McGraw-Hill Companies

Columbus, Ohio

Zip is not last.
Zip is head tug.
It is meant to be.

8

www.sra4kids.com

SRA/McGraw-Hill

A Division of The McGraw-Hill Companies

Copyright © 2002 by SRA/McGraw-Hill.

Send all inquiries to:
SRA/McGraw-Hill
8787 Orion Place
Columbus, OH 43240-4027

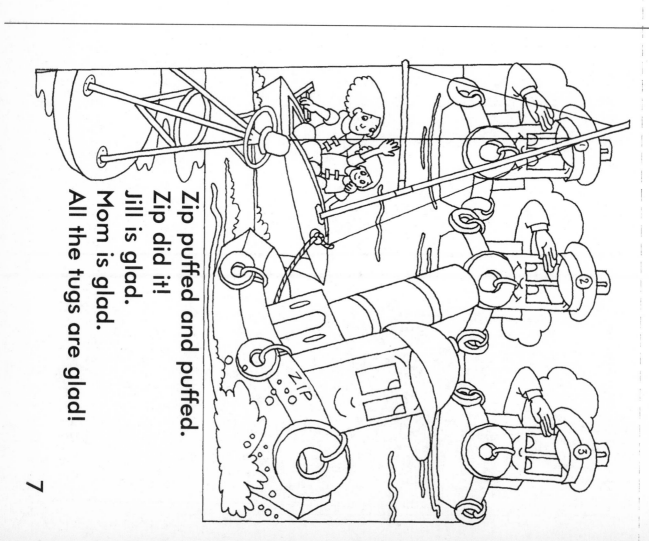

Zip puffed and puffed.
Zip did it!
Jill is glad.
Mom is glad.
All the tugs are glad!

115

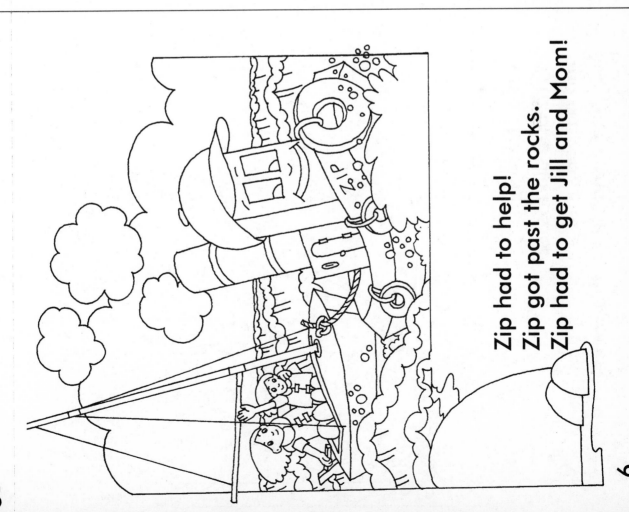

Zip is not a big tug.
Zip is a small tug.
Zip was not the head tug.
Zip was last.

3

Zip had to help!
Zip got past the rocks.
Zip had to get Jill and Mom!

6

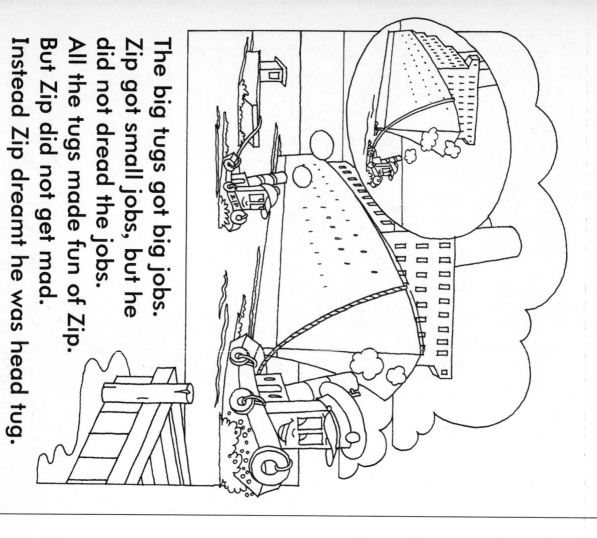

The big tugs got big jobs.
Zip got small jobs, but he
did not dread the jobs.
All the tugs made fun of Zip.
But Zip did not get mad.
Instead Zip dreamt he was head tug.

4

A big storm hit.
Mom and Jill tossed
and dipped.
Will Mom and Jill hit the rocks?

5

117

SRA OPEN COURT READING

Ross's Mess

Practice Book 28

SRA

A Division of The McGraw-Hill Companies
Columbus, Ohio

Tess is back. She is not cross.
Tess missed Ross!

8

2

Ross is stressed.
What a mess!
Will Tess be cross?

7

Tess has a class.
"Do not make a mess, Ross."

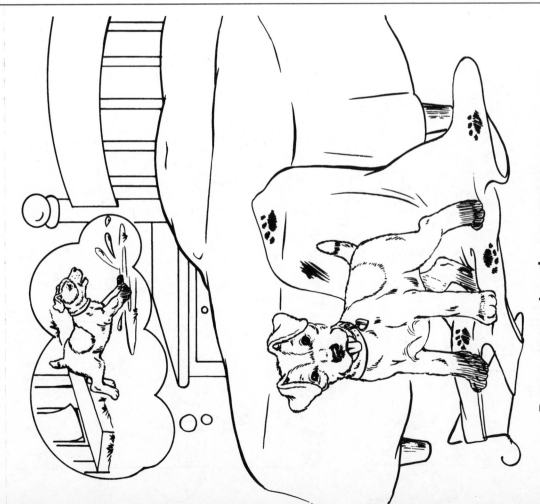

Ross runs in the grass.
Ross steps on Tess's dress.

6

4

Ross cannot sit still.
Ross can toss a ball.

Ross spills a glass.
It makes a mess.

5

SRA OPEN COURT READING

Trish's Ship

Practice Book 29

SRA

A Division of The McGraw-Hill Companies

Columbus, Ohio

Yes! Trish's ship splashes in the sun!

8

www.sra4kids.com

SRA/McGraw-Hill

A Division of The McGraw-Hill Companies

Copyright © 2002 by SRA/McGraw-Hill.

All rights reserved. Except as permitted under the United States Copyright Act, no part of this publication may be reproduced or distributed in any form or by any means, or stored in a database or retrieval system, without prior written permission from the publisher.

Printed in the United States of America.

Send all inquiries to:
SRA/McGraw-Hill
8787 Orion Place
Columbus, OH 43240-4027

Trish calls the ship "The Shellfish."
Can The Shellfish run?

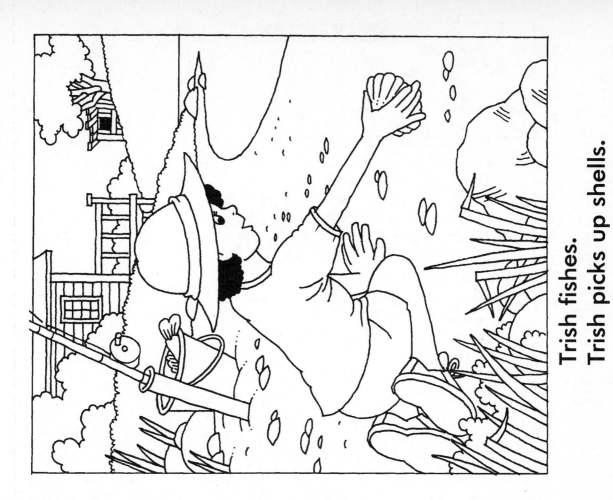

Trish fishes.
Trish picks up shells.

3

Trish has a plan.
Trish gets Mom.
Trish brushes sand from the ship.

6

4

Trish wants a ship.
What is stashed in the shed?

It is a ship!

5

Open Court Reading

Beth Gets a Snack

Practice Book 30

A Division of The McGraw-Hill Companies

Columbus, Ohio

Seth gets in bed.
Beth is not thin. Beth is fat.
Beth is stuffed with thick red thread!

8

125

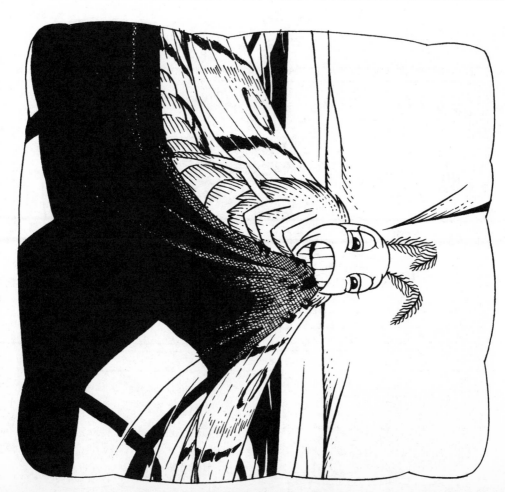

Beth is thrilled with Seth's bedspread.
Beth has this fabric for a snack!

Beth is a bug.
Beth is too thin.
Beth wants a snack.

3

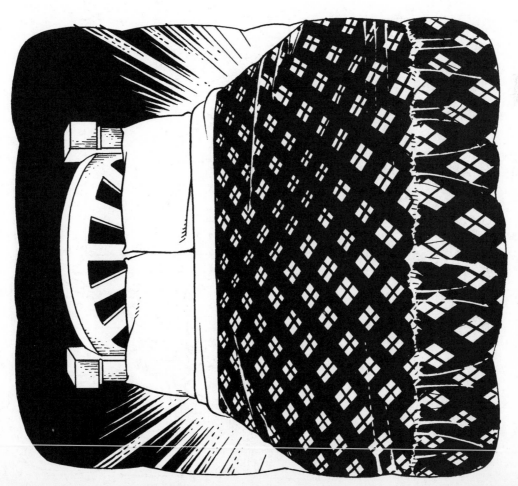

Seth has a bedspread.
This bedspread has thick red threads.

6

Beth wants fabric for a snack.
But where will Beth get fabric?

This is Seth.
Seth gets a bath.

The Animal in the Closet

SRA OPEN COURT READING

Practice Book 31

SRA

A Division of The McGraw-Hill Companies

Columbus, Ohio

"Where is Trisha, Fred? Is Trisha the animal in the closet? Trisha, get to bed."

8

www.sra4kids.com

SRA/McGraw-Hill

A Division of The McGraw-Hill Companies

Copyright © 2002 by SRA/McGraw-Hill.

Printed in the United States of America.

Send all inquiries to:
SRA/McGraw-Hill
8787 Orion Place
Columbus, OH 43240-4027

2

"What can I do? I do not want an animal in my closet."

7

"Mom! Mom! This is a problem.
A big animal is in my closet.
It is as big as a panda!
No. It is as big as a dragon!"

3

lentils

"Will it get out if it has a melon?
Or a banana?
Does it like lentils?"

6

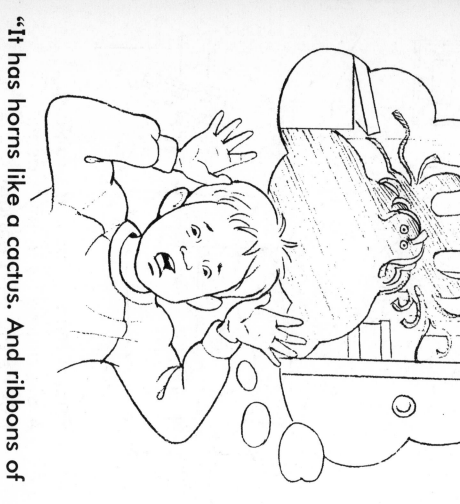

"It has horns like a cactus. And ribbons of metal on its head."

4

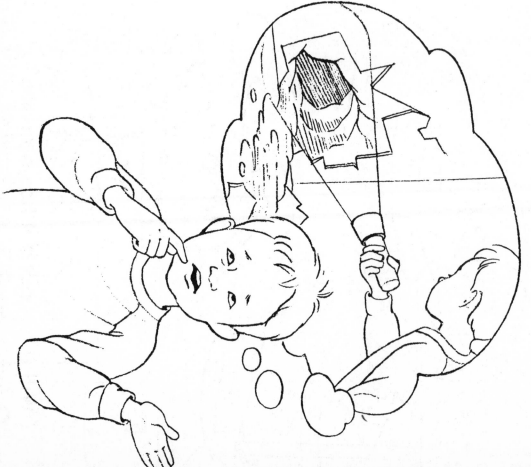

"Did it dig a path to my closet?"

5

SRA Open Court Reading

Lunch on the Porch

Practice Book 32

SRA

A Division of The McGraw-Hill Companies

Columbus, Ohio

133

Lunch on the porch was such a good plan.

8

www.sra4kids.com

SRA/McGraw-Hill

A Division of The McGraw-Hill Companies

Copyright © 2002 by SRA/McGraw-Hill.

Printed in the United States of America.

Send all inquiries to:
SRA/McGraw-Hill
8787 Orion Place
Columbus, OH 43240-4027

Mom chopped up a bunch of chicken strips. Rich and Chad munch on banana chips, crunch on corn, and chug chilled water.

"Can I have lunch?" said Chad.
"Can I have lunch?" said Rich.

3

Rich can sit on this chest.
Chad can sit on this bench.

6

Mom said, "You can have lunch on the porch."

4

"Lunch on the porch?"

5

SRA Open Court Reading

SRA Open Court Reading

Patch Helps

Practice Book 33

SRA

A Division of The McGraw-Hill Companies

Columbus, Ohio

Mitch is glad.
Dad is glad.
Patch gets a snack and
a pat on the head.

8

www.sra4kids.com

SRA/McGraw-Hill

A Division of The McGraw-Hill Companies

Send all inquiries to:
SRA/McGraw-Hill
8787 Orion Place
Columbus, OH 43240-4027

2

Patch catches on.
Patch pulls the truck out of the mud.

7

138

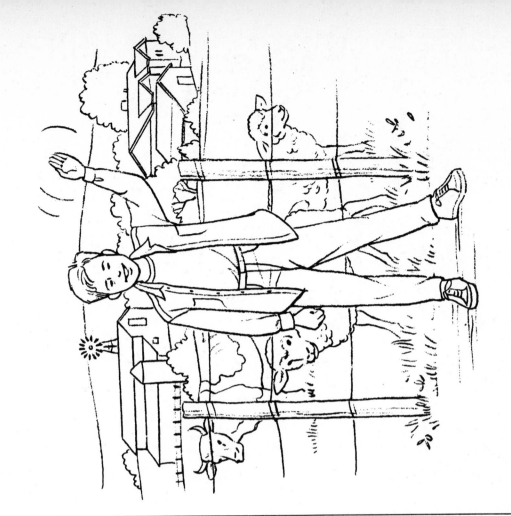

This is Mitch.
Mitch is on a ranch.

3

What is this?
The truck is stuck in mud!
"Mitch, fetch Patch. Patch can help."

6

4

Mitch helps Dad hitch up to the truck.

Dad runs the truck, and Mitch
checks the hens.
This one hatched!

5

SRA Open Court Reading

At the Farm

Practice Book 34

A Division of The McGraw-Hill Companies

Columbus, Ohio

"This is Gran and Gramps's farm, Darla. You can help on the farm on this trip."

3

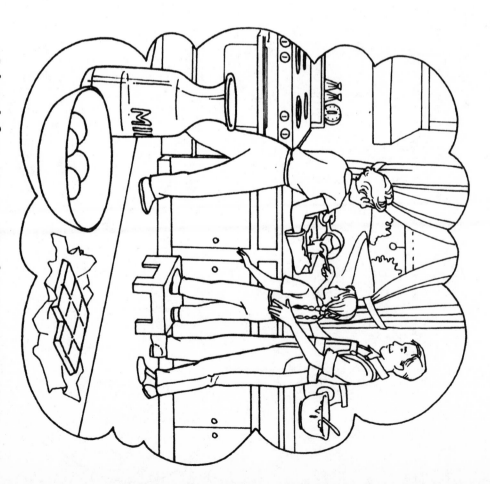

"I had fun, too, Darla. I got to help make fudge. Mmmmm! Such rich fudge. It was fun."

7

143

"Mom, what was it like on a farm?" Darla asked.

"I had hard jobs. I had to start after the alarm buzzed. I did my part."

"Then I helped in the barn."

6

"I helped Dad plant a garden, Darla.
I planted corn and parsnips."

4

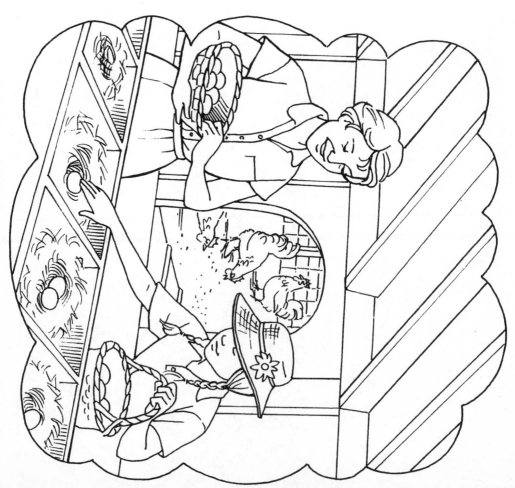

"I helped Mom with the chickens.
I got the eggs."

5

SRA Open Court Reading

Lora Lamb

Practice Book 35

A Division of The McGraw-Hill Companies

Columbus, Ohio

I am Lora Lamb.
I am a puppet.

8

2

I can pet a dog.
I am soft.

7

I am Lora Lamb.
I am small.
I cannot think, but I am not dumb.

3

I can pick up crumbs.

6

147

I can do what you can do with the help of a thumb.

4

I can grab a limb.

5

149

OPEN COURT READING

Wes Gets Wet

Practice Book 36

SRA

A Division of The McGraw-Hill Companies

Columbus, Ohio

The truck is scrubbed. The twig went away.
But Wes is wet. Wilma is wet, too.

8

2

The wind grabs a twig!
Wes cannot sit by the wall.
Wes jumps up and runs.
Wes is swift.

7

Wilma scrubs Dad's truck.
Wes wants to help.

3

Wes sits by the wall.

6

"Wes, sit by the wall. I do not want you to get all wet."

4

Wilma waxes the truck.

5

SRA Open Court Reading

Wilma's Cat

Practice Book 37

A Division of The McGraw-Hill Companies

Columbus, Ohio

"Watch this!" said Wilma.

"It is not a whim. Whip likes his snacks."

8

153

www.sra4kids.com

SRA/McGraw-Hill

A Division of The McGraw-Hill Companies

Copyright © 2002 by SRA/McGraw-Hill.

All rights reserved. Except as permitted under the United States Copyright Act, no part of this publication may be reproduced or distributed in any form or by any means, or stored in a database or retrieval system, without prior written permission from the publisher.

Printed in the United States of America.

Send all inquiries to:
SRA/McGraw-Hill
8787 Orion Place
Columbus, OH 43240-4027

2

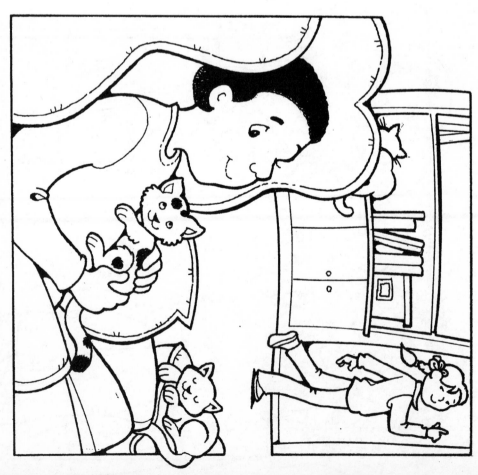

"Well, when Whip gets a whiff of cat snacks, he runs fast. Whip runs past fast to get the snacks."

7

"Where is Whip the cat?" asked Wilma.

3

"You call him Whip? That is odd."

6

4

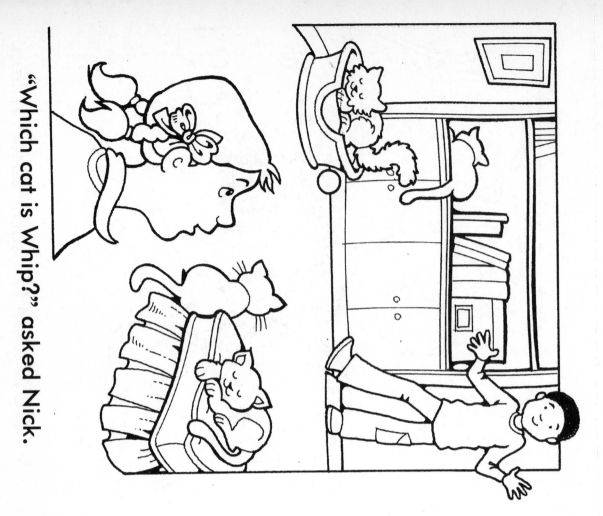

"Which cat is Whip?" asked Nick.

"Whip is the small tan cat with
black spots," said Wilma.
"There he is!"

5

SRA Open Court Reading

Chandler Gets Under

Practice Book 38

SRA

A Division of The McGraw-Hill Companies

Columbus, Ohio

Chandler is under Amber's bed!

8

157

www.sra4kids.com

SRA/McGraw-Hill

A Division of The McGraw-Hill Companies

Copyright © 2002 by SRA/McGraw-Hill.

All rights reserved. Except as permitted under the United States
Copyright Act, no part of this publication may be reproduced or
distributed in any form or by any means, or stored in a database
or retrieval system, without prior written permission from the
publisher.

Printed in the United States of America.

Send all inquiries to:
SRA/McGraw-Hill
8787 Orion Place
Columbus, OH 43240-4027

2

There is a big summer storm.
Thunder crashes.
Where is Chandler? Did the thunder
bother him?

7

This is Amber and her dog, Chandler.

3

159

Amber and Chandler must get in bed.
Chandler gets under his bedspread. Amber
gets under her bedspread.

6

Chandler likes to be under the steps.

Chandler gets his dinner under the steps.

4

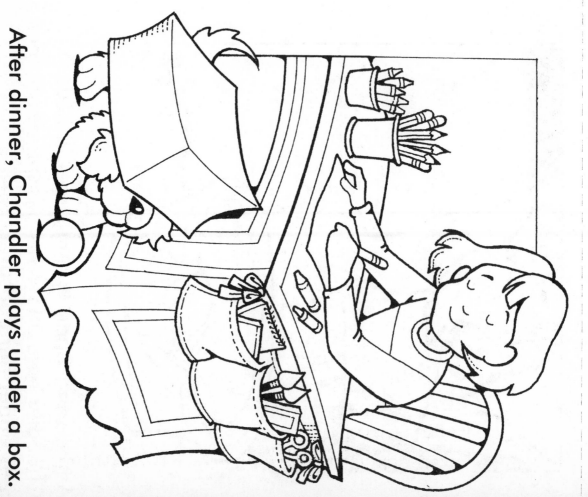

After dinner, Chandler plays under a box.

5

161

SRA OPEN COURT READING

Brenda and the Bird

Practice Book 39

SRA

A Division of The McGraw-Hill Companies
Columbus, Ohio

Mom is firm. "Brenda, you are a girl, not a bird! Now you must have a water bath."

8

2

Brenda gets a dirt bath, too!

7

Brenda has a bird on her shirt.

3

The bird gets a dirt bath.

6

Brenda sees a bird just like the bird
on her shirt!

4

At first Brenda just watches the bird.

5

SRA Open Court Reading

Curt the Surfer

Practice Book 40

SRA

A Division of The McGraw-Hill Companies

Columbus, Ohio

Hamburgers

"But hamburgers are not your turf!"

8

www.sra4kids.com

SRA/McGraw-Hill

A Division of The McGraw-Hill Companies

Copyright © 2002 by SRA/McGraw-Hill.

Send all inquiries to:
SRA/McGraw-Hill
8787 Orion Place
Columbus, OH 43240-4027

2

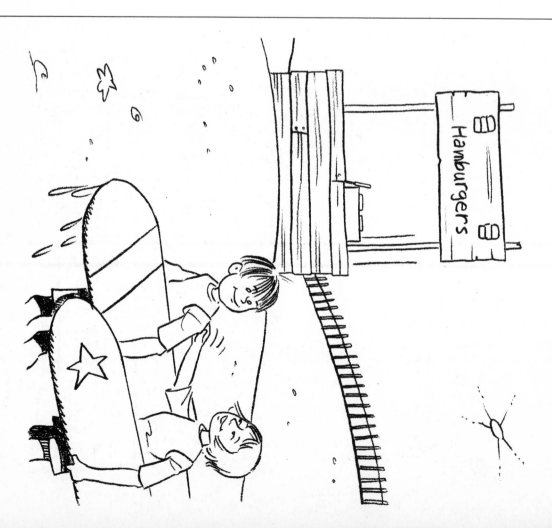

"Yes, Curt, the surf is your turf."

7

This is Curt.
Curt is at the hamburger stand.

3

Curt can surf!
Curt is a blur as he spins and turns.

6

167

This is Erma. Erma can surf. Erma tells Curt, "I am the best surfer."

4

"That is absurd," blurts Curt. "The surf is my turf."

5

SRA Open Court Reading

Turtle's Bundle

Practice Book 41

A Division of The McGraw-Hill Companies

Columbus, Ohio

Don settled his apples, his fiddle, and the rest of his pickle back in his bundle. See you, Don.

8

www.sra4kids.com

SRA/McGraw-Hill

A Division of The McGraw-Hill Companies

Copyright © 2002 by SRA/McGraw-Hill.

All rights reserved. Except as permitted under the United States Copyright Act, no part of this publication may be reproduced or distributed in any form or by any means, or stored in a database or retrieval system, without prior written permission from the publisher.

Printed in the United States of America.

Send all inquiries to:
SRA/McGraw-Hill
8787 Orion Place
Columbus, OH 43240-4027

Then the little turtle felt a gurgle and a rumble in his middle.
I have a pickle.
Mmmm. Don nibbled the pickle.

Don is a little turtle.
Don has a big bundle.
He set the bundle down.

"Want to see a turtle fiddle?" asked Don.
Don dazzled as he fiddled.

4

Don dropped the handle.
He undid the buckle.

"Want to see a turtle juggle?" asked Don.
Don shuffled apples.

SRA Open Court Reading

Satchel's Nickel

Practice Book 42

SRA

A Division of The McGraw-Hill Companies

Columbus, Ohio

Satchel will not spend his nickel on a trip.
Satchel's nickel will go in his pocket.
He will not spend it now.

8

2

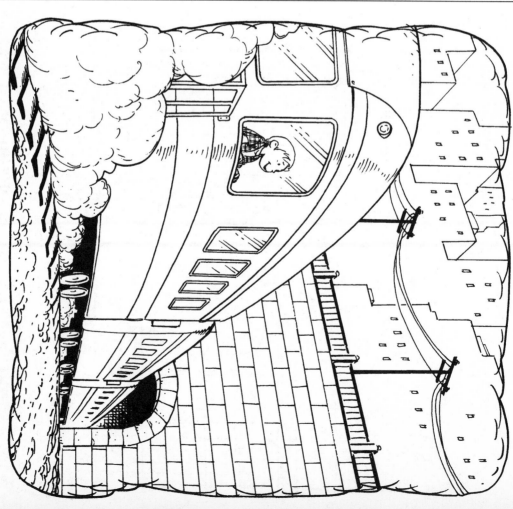

Did he want to go in a tunnel?
Can a nickel get him a trip?

7

Satchel has a nickel.
What can he get with a nickel?

3

Can Satchel get a pet camel?
He can call it Pamela.

6

175

A red flannel jacket?
A hard metal funnel?

A new model car?
Just a bit of tinsel?

SRA OPEN COURT READING

SRA Open Court Reading

SRA Open Court Reading

Breakfast in Bed

Practice Book 43

SRA

A Division of The McGraw-Hill Companies

Columbus, Ohio

"You are the best, Mark and Kim,"
Mom says. "You get a kiss."

8

www.sra4kids.com

SRA/McGraw-Hill

A Division of The McGraw-Hill Companies

Copyright © 2002 by SRA/McGraw-Hill.

All rights reserved. Except as permitted under the United States Copyright Act, no part of this publication may be reproduced or distributed in any form or by any means, or stored in a database or retrieval system, without prior written permission from the publisher.

Printed in the United States of America.

Send all inquiries to:
SRA/McGraw-Hill
8787 Orion Place
Columbus, OH 43240-4027

"Breakfast in bed?" asks Dad.
"Milk, eggs, and dark bread," says Mark.
"I helped," Kim adds.

179

Mark and Kim like the kitchen.

3

Breakfast is set.
"Are you up?" Mark asks.

6

4

Mark works and Kim helps.
They are skilled kids.

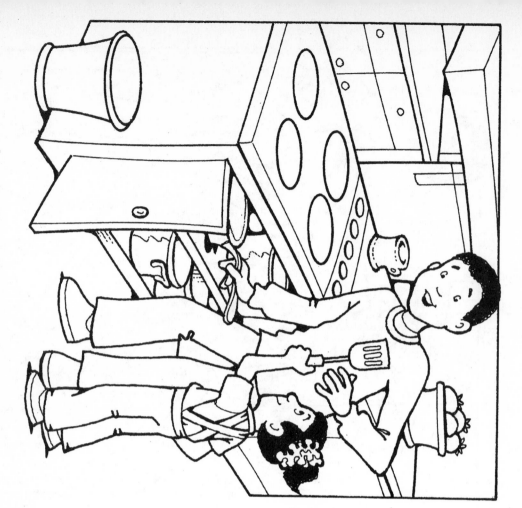

Mark puts eggs in a skillet.
Kim gets dishes.
Skip the dog watches Mark and Kim.

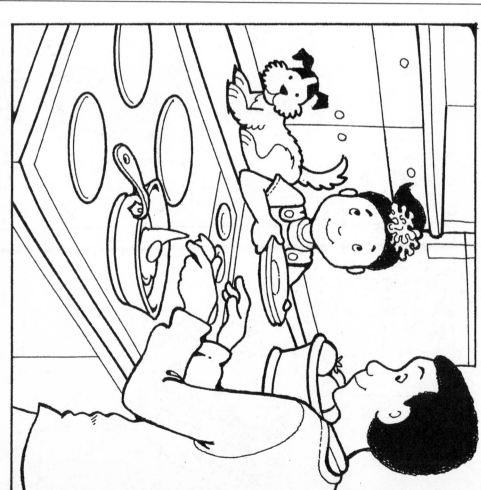

5

SRA Open Court Reading

Ding Dong!

Practice Book 44

SRA

A Division of The McGraw-Hill Companies

Columbus, Ohio

Ring! Ring!
Mom is ringing the dinner bell.
We cannot swing now.

8

2

Fling that thing!
Fetch, King!

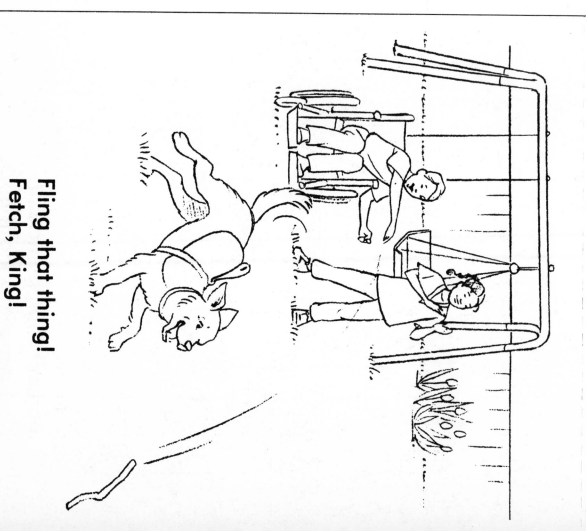

7

183

Ding dong! Ding dong!
Is that the bell?

3

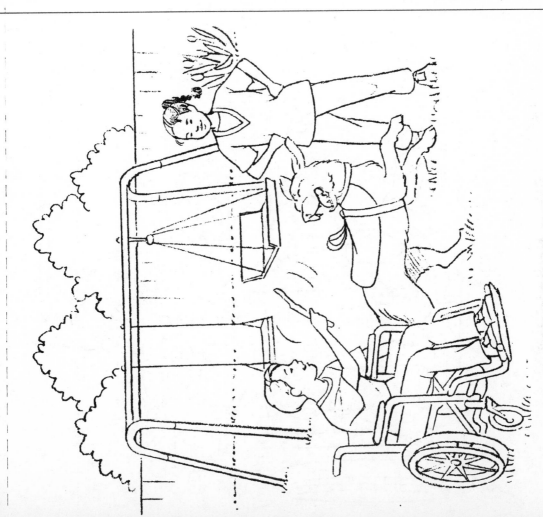

Let's fling a stick.
King will bring it back.

6

4

It is spring.
Want to go swing?

Can I bring King?
He likes playing.

5

The Squirrel Plan

Practice Book 45

SRA

A Division of *The McGraw-Hill Companies*

Columbus, Ohio

Jen's plan was good.

8

www.sra4kids.com

SRA/McGraw-Hill

A Division of The McGraw-Hill Companies

Copyright © 2002 by SRA/McGraw-Hill.

Printed in the United States of America.

Send all inquiries to:
SRA/McGraw-Hill
8787 Orion Place
Columbus, OH 43240-4027

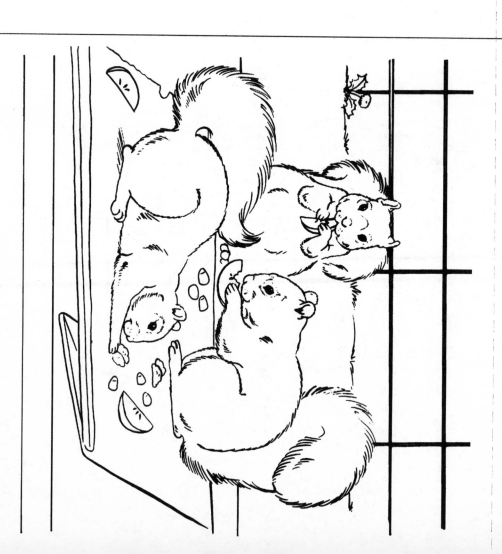

The squirrels quit squirming.
The smart squirrels gobble up the banquet.

7

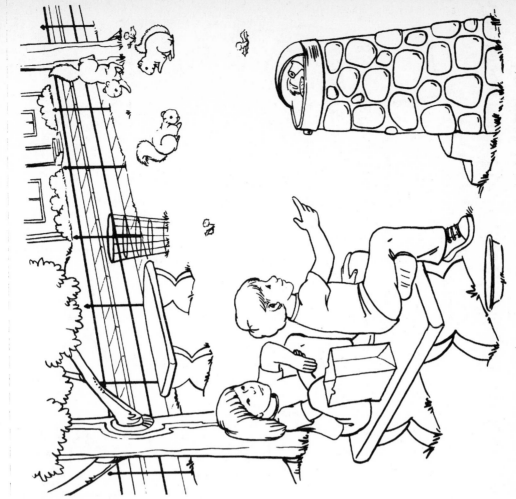

Quentin and Jen squint at the
squirrels in the park.
The squirrels are quick.

3

Quentin wants to help.
He will help quench the squirrels' thirst.
Quentin puts liquid in a pan.
He sets the pan on the aqua bench.

9

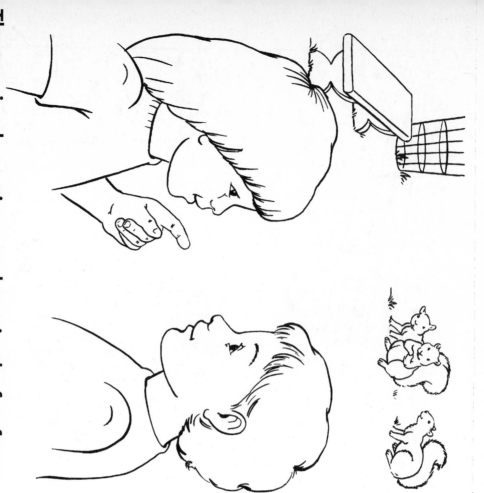

The squirrels squirm and squiggle far from Quentin and Jen.
Jen has a plan.
She will make a banquet for the squirrels.

4

Jen puts corn, apples, and nuts on a bag.
She sets the bag on the aqua bench.

5

SRA Open Court Reading

Beth's Yak

Practice Book 46

SRA
A Division of The McGraw-Hill Companies
Columbus, Ohio

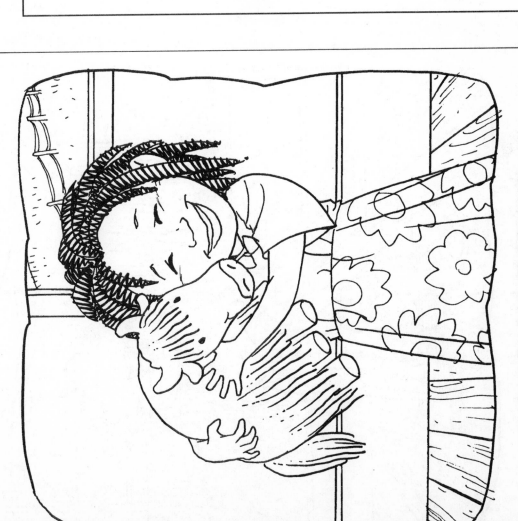

Is Beth's yak the best?
Yes, Beth thinks so.

189

8

www.sra4kids.com

SRA/McGraw-Hill

A Division of The McGraw-Hill Companies

Copyright © 2002 by SRA/McGraw-Hill.

Printed in the United States of America.

Send all inquiries to:
SRA/McGraw-Hill
8787 Orion Place
Columbus, OH 43240-4027

Beth sings to her yak.
Beth does not yell at her yak.

Beth had a big yak.
Beth kept her yak with her.

3

Beth can make a scarf from yarn for her yak.

6

Beth kept her yak on her bed.
Beth kept her yak in her yard.

Beth fed her yak yams and apples.
The yak liked yams and apples. Yum!
The yak did not like grass. Yuck!

5

SRA Open Court Reading

Mabel's Bread

Practice Book 47

A Division of The McGraw-Hill Companies

Columbus, Ohio

At last, Jason runs by her table. Jason sees the big paper and stops.
"I want this bread and that bread and this bread!" Jason thanks Mabel.
Then Jason packs the breads in his backpack. Mabel and Jason are glad that Mabel fixes breads.

8

2

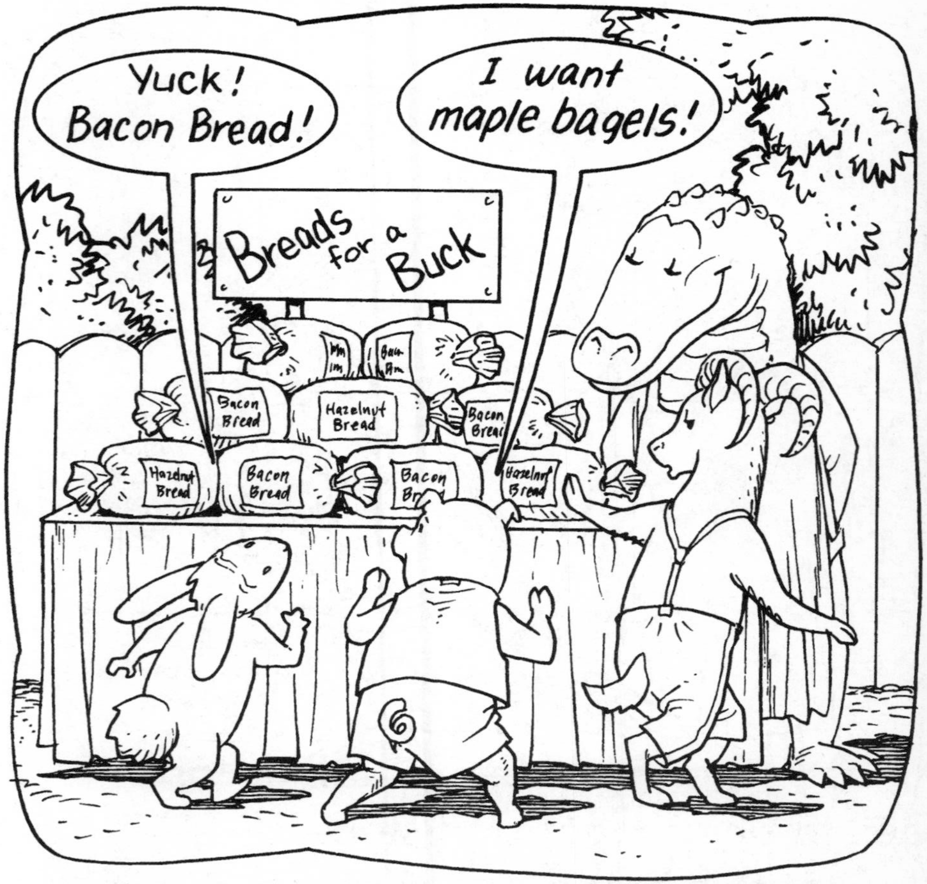

Mabel puts the breads on the table.
She scribbles Breads for a Buck
on chart paper.
Will Mabel be able to sell her breads?

7

194

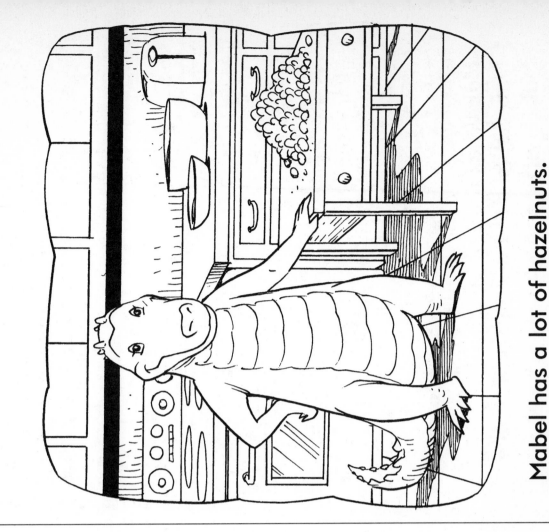

Mabel has a lot of hazelnuts.
Mabel stacks the hazelnuts on a table.

3

Then Mabel puts her breads in plastic.
Mabel gets little bits of paper.
Mabel scribbles on the labels.
The labels stick on the plastic.

6

195

4

Mabel has a lot of bacon.
Mabel stacks the bacon on the table.
Mabel gets her apron.
What will Mabel do?

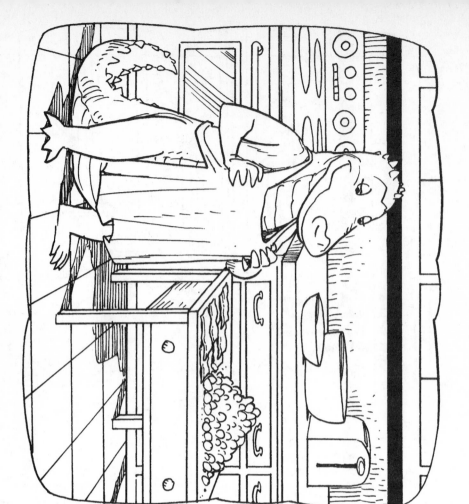

Mabel starts her basic mixing.
Mabel is fixing bacon breads.
She is mixing breads with hazelnuts.
Mabel smells the breads.
"Yum!" utters Mabel.

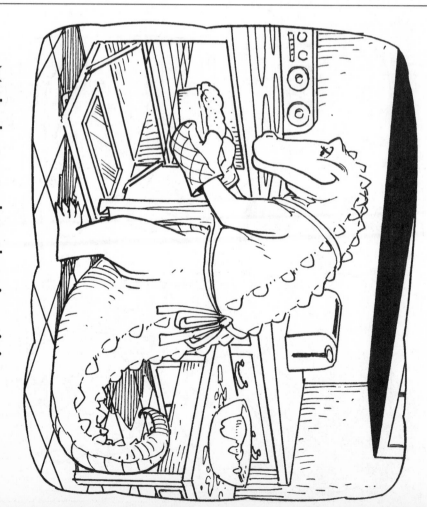

5

SRA OPEN COURT READING

Monster Cake

Practice Book 48

SRA

A Division of The McGraw-Hill Companies

Columbus, Ohio

"What is that?" asked Kate.
"A monster must want this cake!"
"No!" yelled Jake. "No! Not a monster!"

8

"Are you still scared?" asked Kate.

"When was I scared?" asked Jake.

"I was not scared."

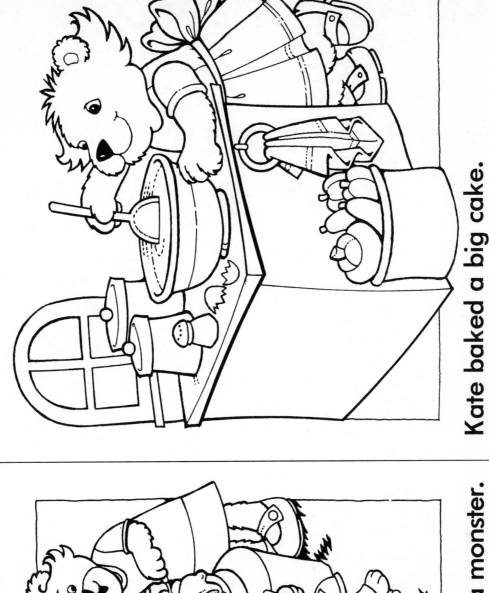

Kate baked a big cake.
"I will take this cake to Jake," said Kate.
Kate made the cake in the shape of a grape.

3

"It is me," said Kate. "I am not a monster.
I baked you a cake."
"You baked me a cake?" asked Jake.
Jake ate a little cake.

6

Kate saw Jake camping in his tent.
Jake was not awake.
"Jake?" said Kate.

4

Jake did not see Kate.
He saw a big dark shape!
Jake started to quake and shake!
"Help!" yelled Jake. "It's a monster!"

5